T0104184

HAPPY HOLIDAYS!

It's the most wonderful time of the year
– curl up and do some doodling.

Doodle By Number™ isn't just for kids, it's for anyone who
wants to quiet their busy thoughts, awaken their creative spirit,
and enjoy the peace that comes with a little mindfulness.
And what better time for a mindful activity than those precious,
peaceful moments of whimsical, wintry wonder.

In the midst of all the celebration, remember the gift of contemplation.
That's why I designed this book: holidays and doodling are a natural fit,
and we could all benefit from more of both.

You don't need to be an artist or an expert to enjoy doodling.
You just need to start moving your pen across the paper, ready to
follow the journey wherever it may lead.

Wishing you a warm and cozy holiday season.

Melissa x

WHY DOODLE?

It's true! People have been doodling for millennia. "Spontaneous drawing" has been studied and verified as a means to decrease stress in our lives.

Taking pen in hand and using the rhythmic motions of doodling, activates the relaxation response within the brain. Just the thing to calm the chaos!

Playfulness
Doodling promotes well-being, allowing you to lighten your mood whenever you feel overwhelmed.

Creative Freedom
Doodling is a workout for the mind that can help you focus on new ideas and bring fresh insights.

Improved Focus
Doodling is a simple and effective way to help you concentrate and process information.

DISCOVER THE BENEFITS OF DOODLING TODAY

Manage Emotions
Doodling is a safe method to evaluate unsettling emotions, converting jumbled feelings into a peaceful state of mind.

Greater Productivity
Doodling can refresh your mind and reset your thoughts, allowing for a greater sense of clarity.

Increased Memory
Studies indicate that while listening to others, the brain can recall 29% more information while doodling.

This Doodle By Number
Belongs To

....

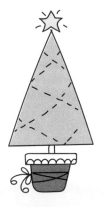

By Doodle Lovely

A holiday is an opportunity to journey within. It is also a chance to chill, to relax. It is when I switch on my rest mode.

PRABHAS

Copyright © 2021 Doodle Lovely Inc.
All rights reserved. This book or any portion thereof may not be reproduced or used in any manner whatsoever without the expressed written permission of the publisher except for the use of brief quotations in a book review. Made in Canada.

How to use your
DOODLE by NUMBER™

Pick up a pen, your favorite marker, or pencil of any color.

At the bottom of each example page there is a selection of five doodle patterns to choose from. Each pattern is circled and numbered.

Follow the numbers to create a doodle pattern on the opposite page. If you want to use more or less doodles, go for it!

Complete the *Doodle By Number*™ and touch it up to your satisfaction.

Feel free to make the doodle your own with your favorite shapes, lines and patterns. Even add color if you like. Doodle-riffic!

Follow the numbers to match your doodles on the opposite page.

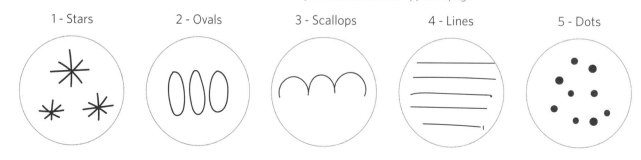

| 1 - Stars | 2 - Ovals | 3 - Scallops | 4 - Lines | 5 - Dots |

Love the giver more than the gift.

BRIGHAM YOUNG

holiday wishes

To:

Follow the numbers to match your doodles on the opposite page.

1 - Snowflakes   2 - Circles   3 - Petal Patterns   4 - Triangles & Circles   5 - Lines

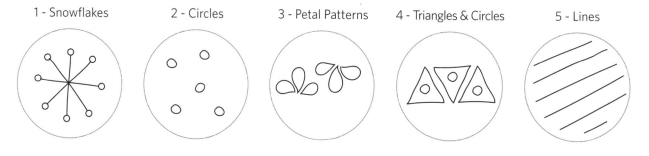

In the still quiet of a cold Christmas night, I feel your spirit warming my heart.

MARIO QUINTANA

Follow the numbers to match your doodles on the opposite page.

1 - Zig Zags	2 - Swirls	3 - Circles	4 - Lines	5 - Wavy Lines

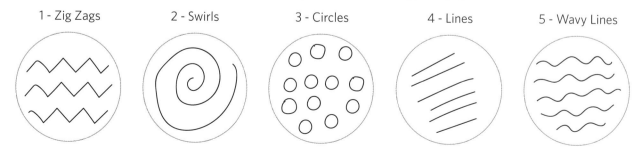

My idea of Christmas, whether old fashioned or modern, is very simple: loving others.

BOB HOPE

Follow the numbers to match your doodles on the opposite page.

1 - Beans   2 - Circles   3 - Scallops & Dots   4 - Stars   5 - Lines

It's the most
wonderful time
of the year.

UNKNOWN

Follow the numbers to match your doodles on the opposite page.

1 - Dots & Circles   2 - Lines & Circles   3 - Swirls   4 - Arcs & Strokes   5 - Lines

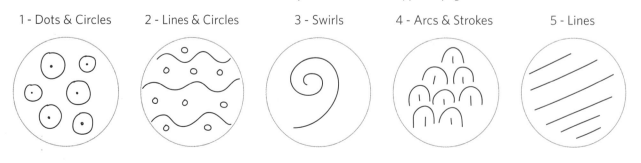

The best way to spread holiday cheer is singing loud for all to hear.

UNKNOWN

Follow the numbers to match your doodles on the opposite page.

1 - Tear Drops 2 - Double Scallops 3 - Circles 4 - X's 5 - Lines

A holiday isn't a holiday without plenty of freedom and fun.

LOUISA MAY ALCOTT

Follow the numbers to match your doodles on the opposite page.

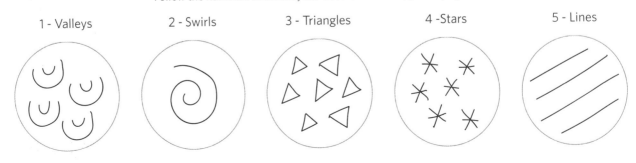

1 - Valleys   2 - Swirls   3 - Triangles   4 - Stars   5 - Lines

Take time to do
what makes your
soul happy.

UNKNOWN

Follow the numbers to match your doodles on the opposite page.

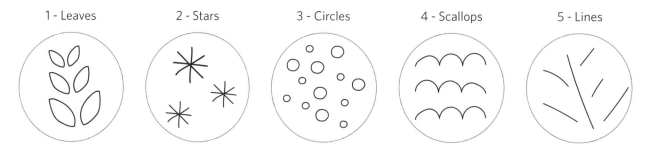

1 - Leaves   2 - Stars   3 - Circles   4 - Scallops   5 - Lines

There's nothing cozier than a Christmas tree all lit up.

JENNY HAN

Follow the numbers to match your doodles on the opposite page.

1 - Circles & Zags   2 - Circles & Strokes   3 - Blanket Stich   4 - Dots   5 - Lines

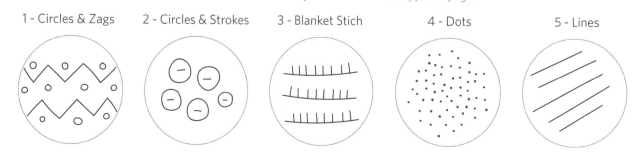

Christmas isn't a season,
it's a feeling.

EDNA FERBER

Follow the numbers to match your doodles on the opposite page.

1 - Bursts   2 - Holly Leaves   3 - Circles   4 - Scallops   5 - Lines

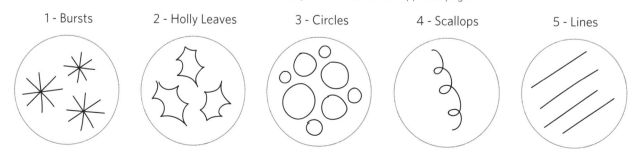

The best Christmas gift is to realize how much you already have.

UNKNOWN

Follow the numbers to match your doodles on the opposite page.

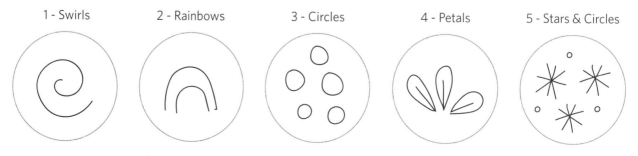

1 - Swirls	2 - Rainbows	3 - Circles	4 - Petals	5 - Stars & Circles

May your walls know joy, may every room hold laughter, and every window open to great possibility.

KATRINA·KENISON

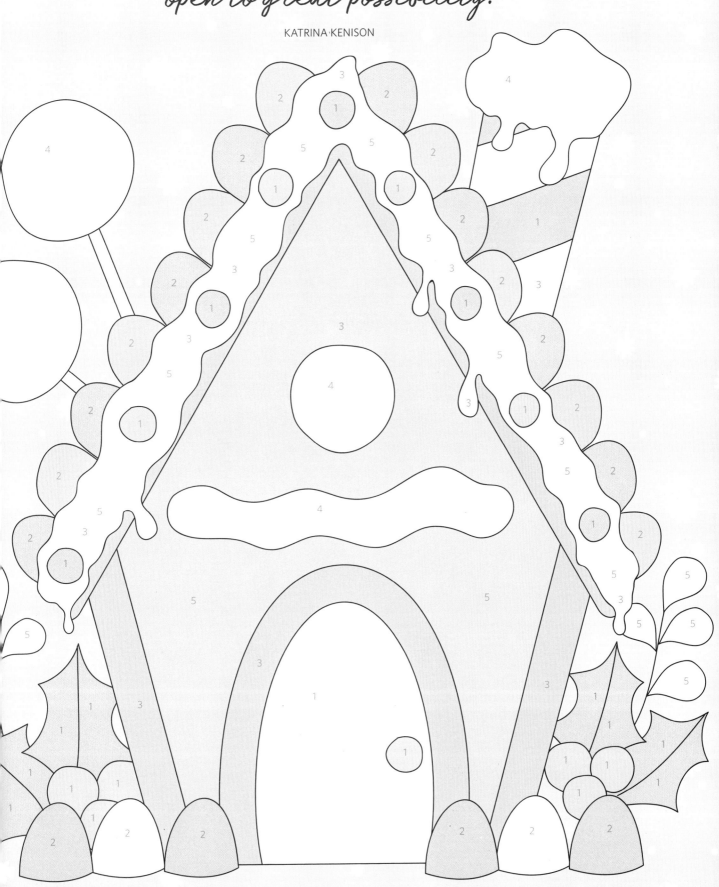

Follow the numbers to match your doodles on the opposite page.

| 1 - Corn Pops | 2 - Circles & Dots | 3 - Lines | 4 - Tear Drops | 5 - Puffs |

Christmas gives us an
opportunity to pause and
reflect on the important
things around us.

DAVID CAMERON

Follow the numbers to match your doodles on the opposite page.

1 - Snowflakes   2 - Lines   3 - Leaves   4 - Zig Zags   5 - Spirals

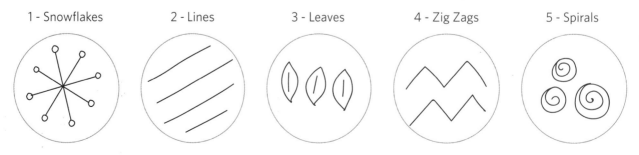

Sleep, breathe, read, doodle, eat, drink, hug, snuggle and be merry.

UNKNOWN

Follow the numbers to match your doodles on the opposite page.

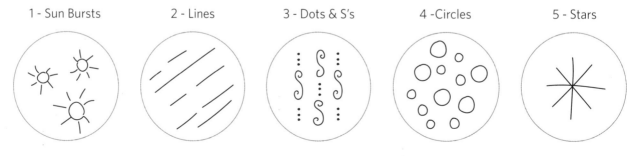

1 - Sun Bursts	2 - Lines	3 - Dots & S's	4 -Circles	5 - Stars

It's time to all in love with Christmas all over again.

UNKNOWN

Follow the numbers to match your doodles on the opposite page.

1 - Puffs   2 - Stars   3 - Sprinkles   4 - Loops   5 - Wavy Lines

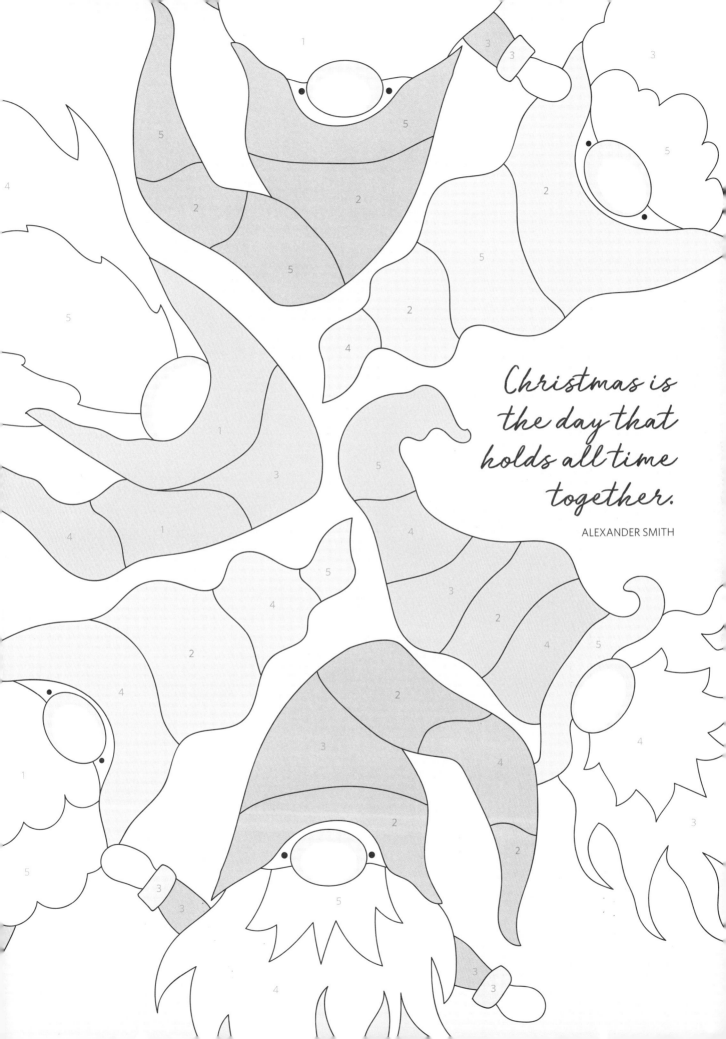

Christmas is the day that holds all time together.

ALEXANDER SMITH

Follow the numbers to match your doodles on the opposite page.

1 - Petal & Scallops   2 - Circle Patterns   3 - Bird Tracks   4 - Dots   5 - Lines

 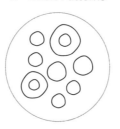  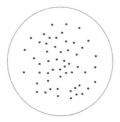 

May your holidays be
wreathed in joy.

UNKNOWN

Follow the numbers to match your doodles on the opposite page.

1 - Circles   2 - Lines   3 - Stars   4 - Dashed Lines   5 - Scallops

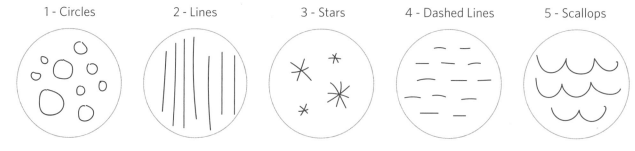

Happiness is there for the taking,
and the making.

OPRAH WINFREY

Follow the numbers to match your doodles on the opposite page.

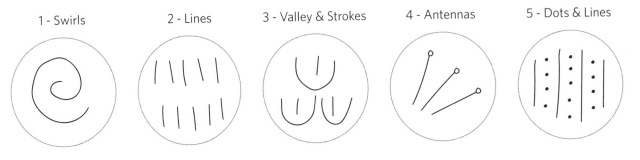

1 - Swirls   2 - Lines   3 - Valley & Strokes   4 - Antennas   5 - Dots & Lines

Solitude is the
soul's holiday.

KATRINA KENISON

Follow the numbers to match your doodles on the opposite page.

1 - Snowflakes   2 - Tents   3 - Scallops   4 - Stars   5 - Lines

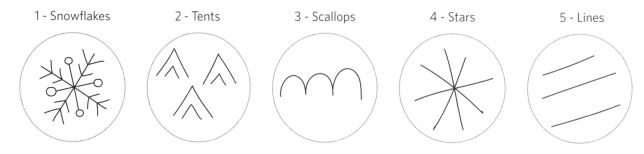

Kindness is like snow. It beautifies everything it covers.

KAHLIL GIBRAN

Follow the numbers to match your doodles on the opposite page.

1 - Circles & Dots   2 - Lines   3 - Wavy Lines   4 - Diamonds   5 - Curves

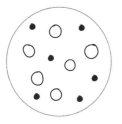

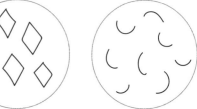

An empty tank
will take
you exactly
nowhere.
Take time
to refuel.

UNKNOWN

Follow the numbers to match your doodles on the opposite page.

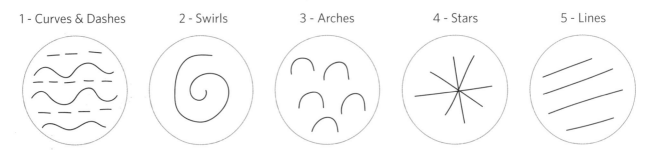

1 - Curves & Dashes   2 - Swirls   3 - Arches   4 - Stars   5 - Lines

May you never
be too grown up to
search the skies
on Christmas Eve.

UNKNOWN

Follow the numbers to match your doodles on the opposite page.

1 - Lines   2 - Flourishes   3 - Circles   4 - Zig Zags   5 - Holly & Berries

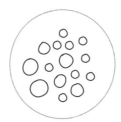

It's not how much we give but how
much love we put into giving.

MOTHER THERESA

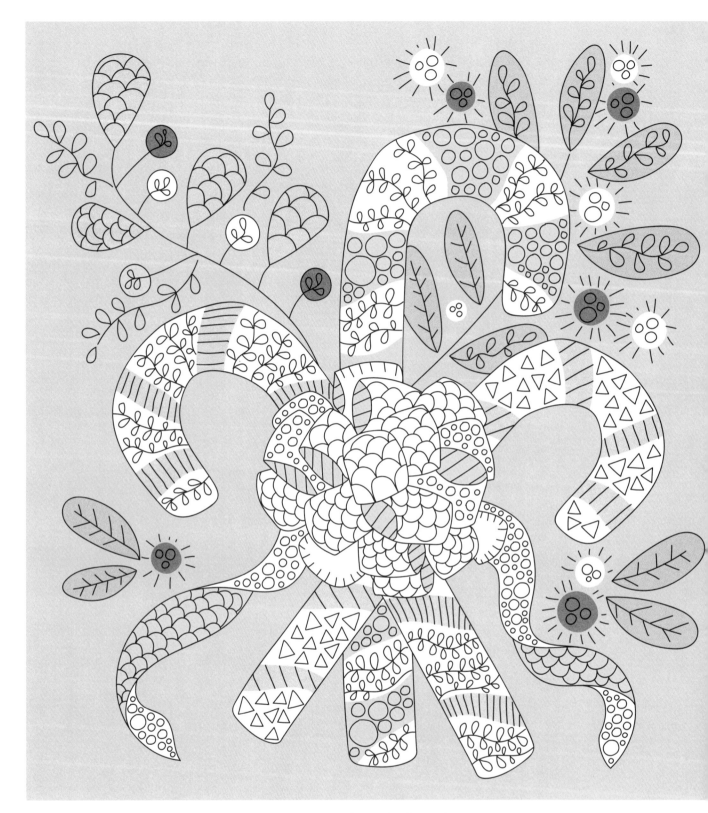

Follow the numbers to match your doodles on the opposite page.

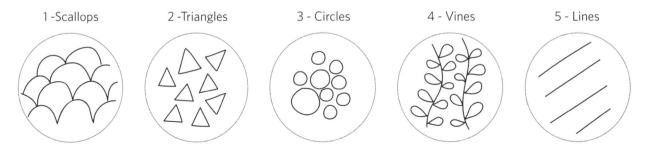

1 -Scallops   2 -Triangles   3 - Circles   4 - Vines   5 - Lines

Do something nice
for you because you
deserve it.

UNKNOWN

Follow the numbers to match your doodles on the opposite page.

1 - Zig Zags & Strokes   2 - Circles   3 - Petal Pattern   4 - Loops   5 - Lines

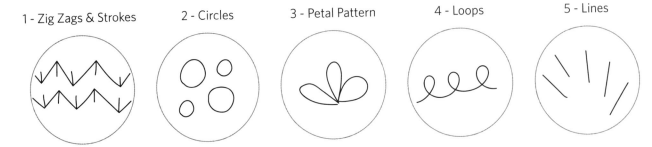

Be happy. Be bright. Be you.

UNKNOWN

Follow the numbers to match your doodles on the opposite page.

1 -Holly & Berries | 2 - Lines | 3 - Zig Zags & V's | 4 - Spirals | 5 - Scallop Antennas

At Christmas, play and make good cheer,
for Christmas comes but once a year.

THOMAS TUSSER

Follow the numbers to match your doodles on the opposite page.

1 - Triangles   2 - Lines   3 - Branches   4 - Stars   5 - Scallops & Circles

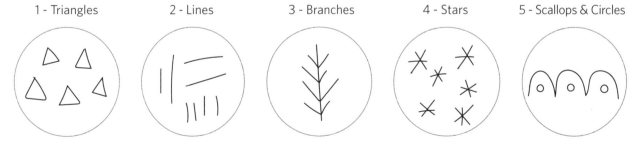

I wish we could put some of the Christmas spirit in jars and open a jar of it every month.

HARLAN MILLER

Follow the numbers to match your doodles on the opposite page.

1 - Lines   2 - Antennas   3 - Swirls   4 - U's   5 - Ornamentals

There are two ways of spreading light: to be the candle or the mirror that reflects it.

EDITH WHARTON

Follow the numbers to match your doodles on the opposite page.

1 - Spirals   2 - Circles   3 - Puffs   4 - X's   5 - Lines

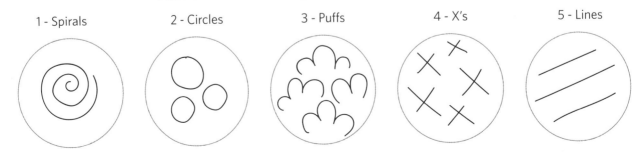

Blessed is the season
which engages
the whole world in
a conspiracy of love.

HAMILTON WRIGHT MAYBI

Follow the numbers to match your doodles on the opposite page.

1 - Strokes & Circles

2 - Petals

3 - Lines

4 - Scallops

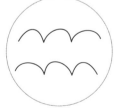

5 - Spirals

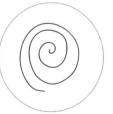

A holiday is a opportunity to journey within.

PRABHAS

Follow the numbers to match your doodles on the opposite page.

1 - Zig Zags	2 - Circles	3 - Lines	4 - Rectangles	5 - Dashes

 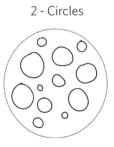  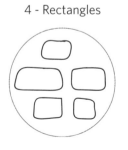 

And now we welcome the new year.
Full of things that have never been.

RAINER MARIA RILKE

Meet the Doodler

MELISSA LLOYD is an international doodler, designer, teacher, author and inspirationalist. Her passion for creativity can be found globally on products, environments and in the hearts of those with whom she has connected.

Melissa combines her twenty plus years of experience in professional design and communication with her passion for humanity, psychology, art therapy and mindfulness; infusing a deep understanding of self.

Melissa teaches soul-care through creative practices and encourages you to learn how to navigate the stormy seas of life, reducing stress and rejuvenating your mind.

By honoring your creative soul and the celebration of living in the moment, Melissa inspires you to bring joy back into your life by finding a place of peace internally. Her transformational approach to creativity, through doodling and living, inspires others to live a healthier and happier life. 'Always Be You... For You.'

Melissa balances her time between mothering, creating, teaching and living in her little Cottage By The Sea. To discover more of Melissa's work visit: **DoodleLovely.com**

A little more sparkle,
a little less stress. This holiday,
I wish you the very best.

RUMI

Did you enjoy this *Doodle By Number*™? We would love to hear your feedback!
Please email us: **hello@doodlelovely.com**

Connect with us to know when the next edition of *Doodle By Number*™
will be available in our online shop.
www.DoodleLovely.com

Doodling to calm the chaos

Doodle Lovely is here to provide soul-care through
creative products so you can live a healthier and happier life.
See some of the other titles in this series below.

BEGINNER - DOODLE BY NUMBER™ SERIES

Beginner Doodle By Number™ - Volume 1

Beginner Doodle By Number™ - For Dog Lovers - Volume 2

Beginner Doodle By Number™ - For Cat Lovers - Volume 3

Beginner Doodle By Number™ - For Botanical Lovers - Volume 4

Beginner Doodle By Number™ - For Holiday Lovers - Volume 5

These and other titles are available from the Doodle Lovely Web Shop.
www.DoodleLovely.com